Spotlight on Australia

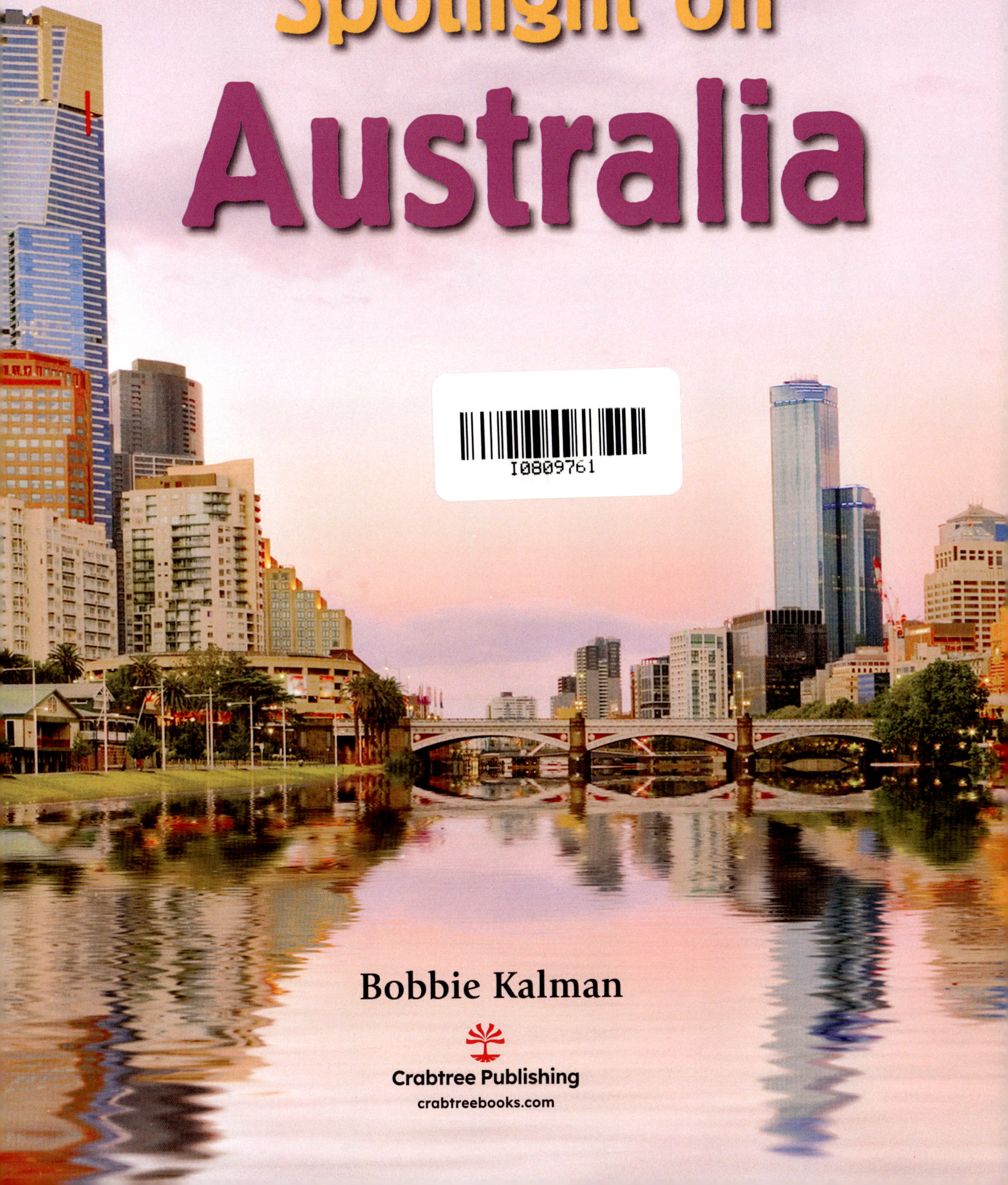

Bobbie Kalman

Crabtree Publishing
crabtreebooks.com

Spotlight On My Country

Created by Bobbie Kalman

For our friend Priscilla Baker, and in memory of Karl Baker, with love from Peter and Bobbie.
We hope this book brings back wonderful memories.

Crabtree Publishing

crabtreebooks.com 800-387-7650

Author and Editor-in-Chief: Bobbie Kalman
Editor: Robin Johnson
Photo research: Bobbie Kalman, Crystal Sikkens
Design: Katherine Kantor, Samantha Crabtree (cover)
Production manager: Candice Campbell
Prepress technician: Katherine Kantor

Hardcover 978-0-7787-3453-6
Paperback 978-0-7787-3479-6
Ebook (pdf) 978-1-4271-0000-0

Printed in the U.S.A./CP082026

Library and Archives Canada Cataloguing in Publication
Kalman, Bobbie, 1947-
Spotlight on Australia / Bobbie Kalman.
(Spotlight on my country)
Includes index.
ISBN 978-0-7787-3453-6 (bound).--
ISBN 978-0-7787-3479-6 (pbk.)
1. Australia--Juvenile literature. I. Title. II. Series.
DU96.K25 2008 j994 C2008-901219-4

Published in Canada
Crabtree Publishing
616 Welland Avenue
St. Catharines, Ontario
L2M 5V6

Published in the United States
Crabtree Publishing
347 Fifth Avenue
Suite 1402-145
New York, NY 10016

Illustrations:
Barbara Bedell: page 15
Katherine Kantor: pages 4, 5, 6, 8, 10, 18, 24
Robert MacGregor: page 12

Photographs:
© BigStockPhoto.com: pages 7 (top), 19 (top right), 25 (middle)
© Dreamstime.com: pages 19 (bottom left except inset), 28 (top left)
© iStockphoto.com: pages 7 (bottom), 16 (bottom right), 17 (except bottom left), 27 (bottom left), 29 (top right)
© 2008 Jupiterimages Corporation: pages 16 (middle right), 20 (top), 21, 25 (top right), 31 (bottom right)
© Shutterstock.com: back cover, pages 1, 3, 5, 8, 9, 10, 11, 12, 13, 14, 15, 16 (top left and bottom left), 17 (bottom left), 18 (background), 19 (background, bottom left inset, and bottom right), 20 (bottom), 22, 23, 24, 25 (top left and bottom), 26, 27 (except bottom left), 28 (bottom left and right), 29 (except top right), 30, 31 (top and bottom left)
Other images by Digital Stock and Digital Vision

Library of Congress Cataloging-in-Publication Data
Kalman, Bobbie.
Spotlight on Australia / Bobbie Kalman.
p. cm. -- (Spotlight on my country)
Includes index.
ISBN-13: 978-0-7787-3479-6 (pbk. : alk. paper)
ISBN-10: 0-7787-3479-X (pbk. : alk. paper)
ISBN-13: 978-0-7787-3453-6 (reinforced library binding : alk. paper)
ISBN-10: 0-7787-3453-6 (reinforced library binding : alk. paper)
1. Australia--Juvenile literature. I. Title.
DU96.K36 2008
994--dc22

2008006378

Contents

Land down under

Australia is a **country**. A country is an area of land with people. A country has **laws**, or rules, that its people must follow. A country also has **borders** that separate it from other countries. Australia does not need borders. It has **oceans** all around it. Oceans are huge areas of salty water. There are also many **seas** around Australia. A sea is a small part of an ocean that has land around it.

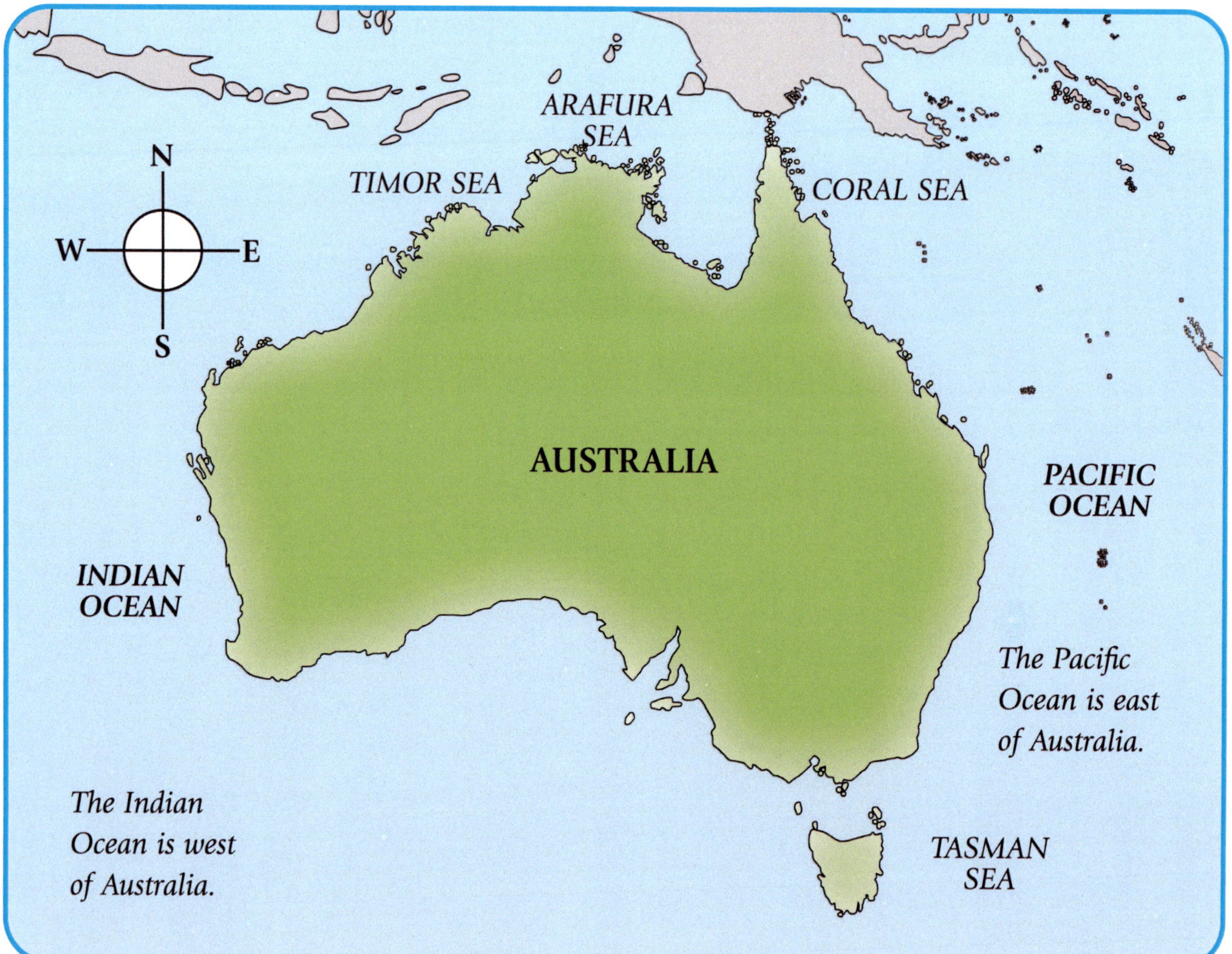

The Pacific Ocean is east of Australia.

The Indian Ocean is west of Australia.

At the bottom of Earth

Australia is part of the **continent** of Australia and Oceania. A continent is a huge area of land. Australia is called the "land down under." It is below the **equator**. The equator is an imaginary circle around the middle of Earth. The equator divides Earth into two parts. Australia is in the bottom part of Earth, called the **Southern Hemisphere**.

This girl is pointing to Australia. Australia is at the bottom of the globe.

There are seven continents on Earth. They are Australia and Oceania, North America, South America, Europe, Asia, Africa, and Antarctica. The smallest continent is Australia and Oceania. Find it on this map of Earth.

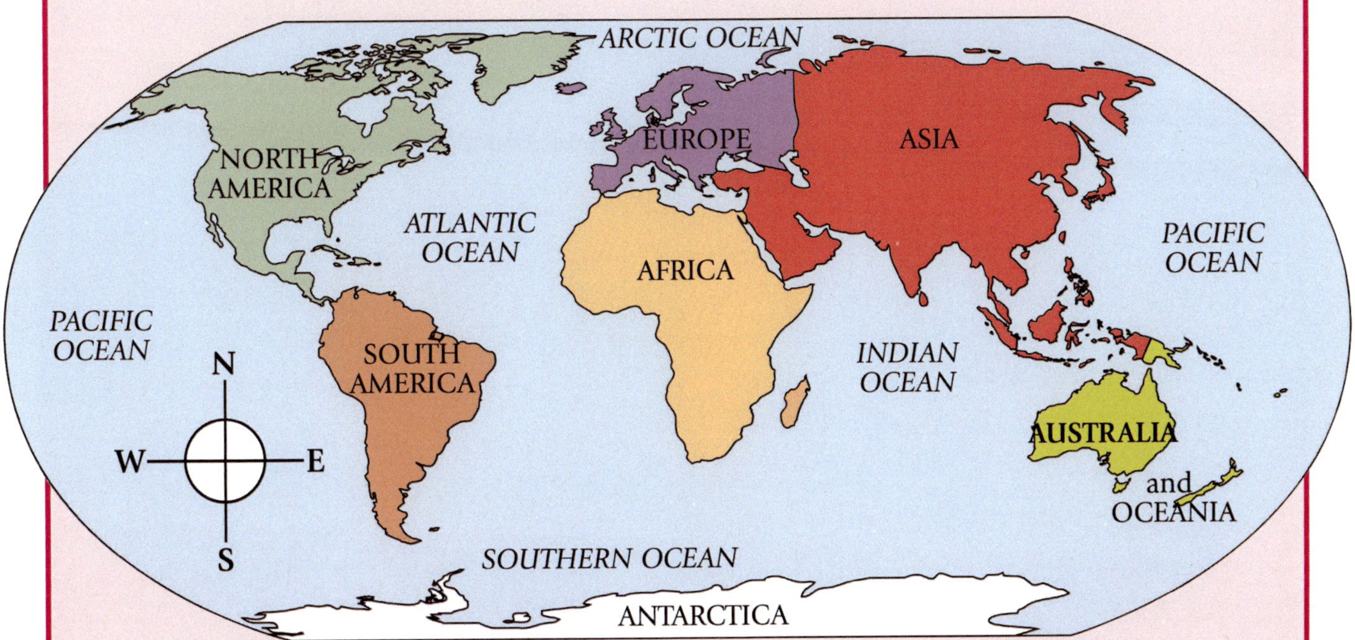

States and territories

Australia is made up of a **mainland** and many **islands**. The mainland is the large land area of Australia. Australia has six **states**, two mainland **territories**, and some smaller territories. A state is an area of a country that has its own **government**. A government makes laws and important decisions for its people. A territory is an area that is run by a country's **federal**, or main, government. Australian Capital Territory and Northern Territory are like states. They have their own governments.

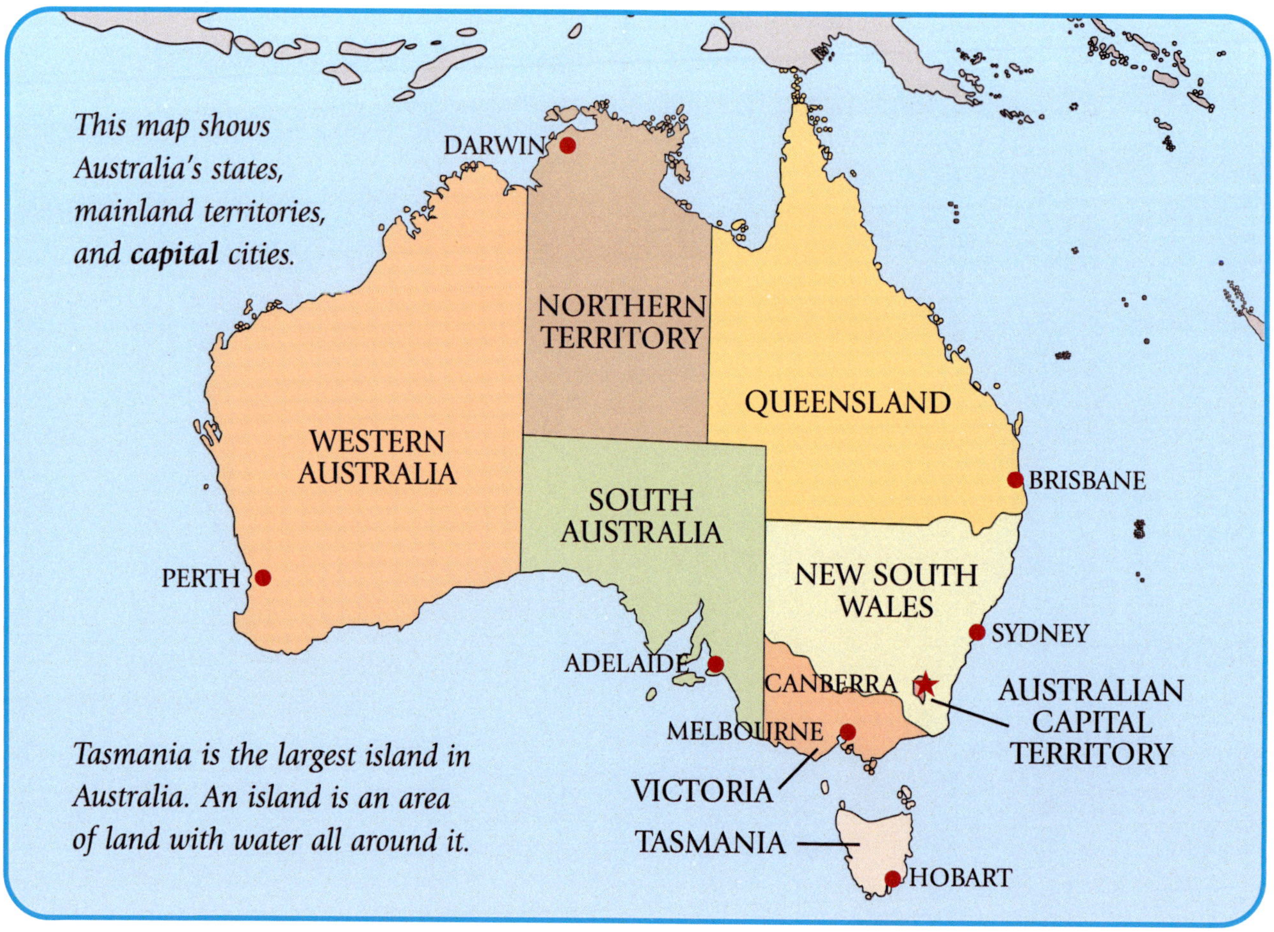

This map shows Australia's states, mainland territories, and ***capital*** *cities.*

Tasmania is the largest island in Australia. An island is an area of land with water all around it.

A long coast

Australia's mainland has **coasts** all around it. A coast is an area where land meets an ocean. Australia's coasts have long sandy beaches, rocky shores, and **cliffs**. Cliffs are tall, steep rocks. Australia's big cities are found along its coasts. The city in the picture below is Sydney.

The Twelve Apostles are ***pillars****, or tall rocks. They were once part of the cliffs on the coast of Victoria. The pillars were cut away from the cliffs by ocean waves and wind.*

Sydney is a big city on Australia's east coast. Its ***harbor*** *is crowded with many boats.*

Life in the oceans

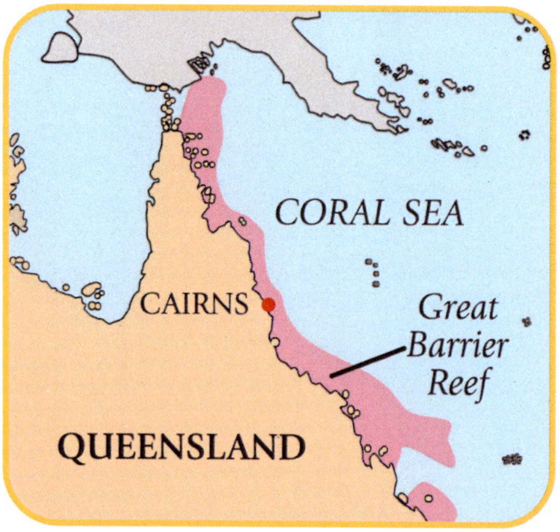

The largest coral reef on Earth is the Great Barrier Reef. It is the area on this map that is shown in pink.

Many kinds of animals live in the oceans around Australia. Some live in **coral reefs**. Coral reefs are huge underwater structures found near coasts. They look like rocks with plants growing on them, but they are not rocks or plants. Coral reefs are made up of groups of tiny animals called **coral polyps**.

More than 350 kinds of sharks live in the Great Barrier Reef. Many other kinds of fish and sea creatures also live in the reef. The sharks eat the smaller fish.

Blue-spotted rays live in the Great Barrier Reef.

Dolphins swim and play in and above the reef.

Sea turtles live in the Great Barrier Reef.

Clownfish and sea anemones live in the reef.

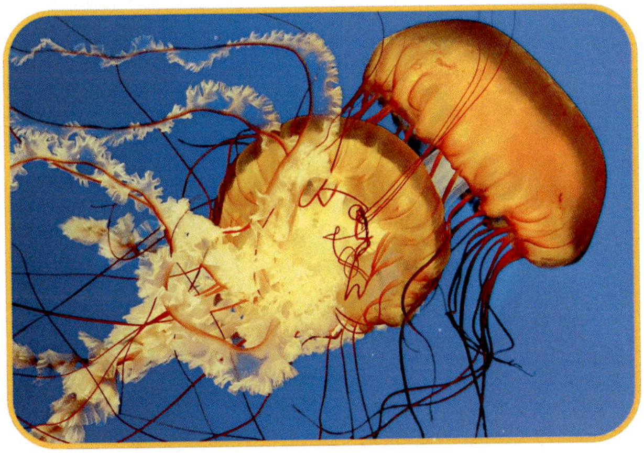

Sea jellies of all kinds live in the oceans around the reefs. These jellies are called sea nettles.

Many people ***scuba dive*** *in the Great Barrier Reef. Does this diver know that he has company?*

Australia's land

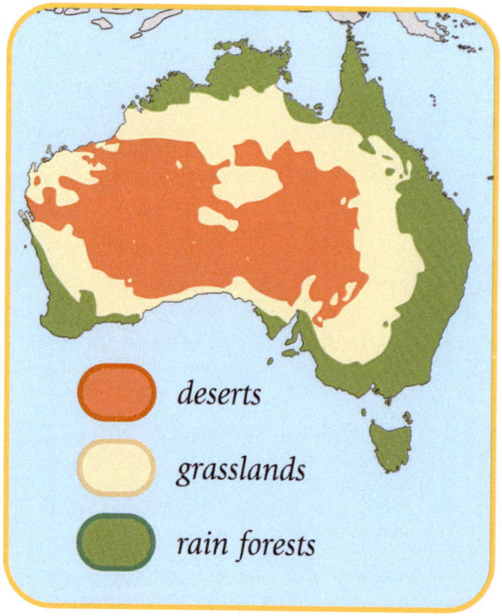

Australia has different **landscapes**. A landscape is how land looks. The middle part of Australia is made up of dry, hot areas called **deserts**. Around the deserts are **grasslands**. Grasslands have long grasses with bushes and some trees. Near the coasts of Australia, there are **rain forests**. There are mountains throughout Australia.

Tropical *rain forests grow in the northern part of Australia. Tropical means hot and* ***humid****, or wet. In the north, the weather is always hot. It rains a lot for half of the year.*

Cooler in the south

Most of Australia is warm all year long. Victoria, Tasmania, and parts of New South Wales are cooler than the rest of the country is, however. They even get some snow in winter.

The Cradle Mountains in Tasmania have snow on their tops in winter.

The Greater Blue Mountains Area is in New South Wales. It has tall cliffs, deep ***valleys****, caves, and* ***swamps****. It also has interesting* ***rock formations****. (See page 13.) The three rocks below are called the Three Sisters.*

Life in the "outback"

The "**outback**" is an area of land that stretches across most of Australia. It is made up mainly of deserts. Very few people live in this hot, dry area of the country. Many kinds of animals live in the outback, however.

Bearded dragons are lizards that live in the outback. They find plants and insects to eat there.